WOKE BABIES®

FEMI and the Mindfulness Machine

Written by **FLO FIELDING**

Illustrated by **SAWYER CLOUD**

Femi was working on a project
for the science fair at school.

"I need pens for planning, tools for building,
and LOTS of time for testing,"
said Femi.

Soon, the project was finished.

"What is it?" asked Grandma.

"It's a wind machine," said Femi.

"When you blow the pinwheel, the blades spin around and create enough power to lift the paper cup."

"Wow!" said Grandma.

But Femi felt sad because sometimes the wind machine worked. And sometimes...

it didn't.

"Does it matter if the wind machine
doesn't lift the cup every time?"
asked Grandma.

"Miss King says that the different parts of a machine work together to DO something, so I think it does matter. I'm blowing as hard as I can, but I need more power."

Femi was quiet at bedtime, but his thoughts buzzed.

"What if my wind machine doesn't work tomorrow, Grandma?
What if I'm too nervous to explain?
And what if Miss King thinks that I didn't try hard enough?"

"Calm yourself," said Grandma.
"Hurry, hurry has no blessings."

"What does that mean?" asked Femi.

"Come downstairs and I'll show you,"
said Grandma.

Grandma started making her special hot chocolate.

"Why does your hot chocolate always taste so good, Grandma?" asked Femi.

"My first secret is science. I pour the hot chocolate from one mug to another so it picks up cold air, which cools the drink down perfectly."

"What's the second secret?" Femi asked.

"Hurry, hurry has no blessings," uttered Grandma.

"As I make it, I take my time. When we feel anxious, slowing down and paying attention to our thoughts can help us feel better

—it's called mindfulness."

"Sometimes, I take deep breaths in and out
to help me relax, too," continued Grandma.
"The best way to tackle ANY problem
is to breathe slowly and stay calm.

Right. It's time to taste it."

Femi gripped the warm mug and watched the frothy bubbles ping and pop before he slowly took a sip.

"MMMmmm!
Slowing down makes it taste better, too!"

"Sometimes Femi,
it's not what you do,
but the way you do it,"
said Grandma with a wink.

On the morning of the science fair, Femi felt strange.

"My legs are too wobbly to walk to school.
My hands are too hot to carry the wind machine.
Can I stay at home with you today, Grandma?"

Grandma put the wind machine into a big box.

"Feeling nervous is normal,"
she said.

"It shows that your body is ready for a challenge.
Don't forget to breathe slowly and stay calm.
Blowing bubbles can help slow down breathing,
too, so I've put some bubbles in your pocket,
just in case you need them."

At school, the gymnasium was split into four zones for the science fair—one for each class. All the children were very excited.

"Femi!" called Jayden.
"Your table is next to mine."

"Wow! That volcano is awesome!" said Femi.

As Femi lifted the wind machine out of the box,
Jayden came over and prodded it.

"What does this do?"
Jayden asked.

His tummy fluttered.
He wanted to go home.

Femi blew the wind machine.
Nothing happened.

Then he remembered what Grandma had taught him.
Femi took a deep breath.

A few minutes later, Femi was feeling a lot better. Grandma's deep breathing really did work, even if his wind machine didn't.

As Miss King moved toward Femi's zone of the gymnasium, some of his classmates started to feel anxious.

"I am so nervous, I feel sick," said Pui.

"What if Miss King doesn't like my project," said Farida anxiously.

"I completely forgot about the science fair and I have NOTHING to present!" said Max as he burst into tears.

Femi reached into his pocket, took
a slow, deep breath, and thought hard.

"Quick everyone, gather round.
I have an idea," he said.

"Okay guys, this is the plan..." said Femi excitedly.

When Miss King finally reached Femi's table, she got a BIG surprise.

"Welcome to our science project!"
announced Femi.

"We are practicing **mindfulness**

by breathing in...

1... 2... 3... 4... 5... and then breathing...

out, 1... 2... 3... 4... 5...
Welcome to the
mindfulness machine,"
said Femi excitedly.

As Femi and his friends blew out, hundreds of tiny bubbles streamed into the air, and something small and amazing whizzed into life, too.

It was...

the wind machine!

While Miss King looked at the last few tables, the rest of Femi's class crowded around him.

"How does it work?" asked Jack.

"Can I join the mindfulness machine?" said Leila.

"Me too!"
"And me!"
insisted the others.

"Everyone is welcome," said Femi.

Soon, it was time for Miss King to give out the prizes.

"Third Prize goes to Jayden for his baking soda volcano.
Second Prize goes to Iris for her water filtering tower.

And First Prize goes to...

Femi and his team for
the magnificent

mindfulness machine!"

Miss King continued, "We have been learning that a machine
has different parts that work together to perform a task.
It was a brilliant idea to involve your classmates as the 'parts'
of your machine, and create both mindfulness AND wind power.

Good job, Femi!
Excellent teamwork,
everyone!"

When Grandma came to pick up Femi, she admired his first prize sticker.

"Did the wind machine work then?" she asked.

"It did," said Femi.
"But wait until you hear where
the wind power came from AND
what I did with the bubbles!
Oh, and Grandma, you were right
about what you said, too."

"Really?" said Grandma, smiling.
"What was that?"

"Sometimes, it's not what you DO, it's the way that you do it!"

About the illustrator

Sawyer Cloud is a self-taught illustrator living in Madagascar, her birth country. She is a passionate artist and has illustrated more than 20 other children's books. Sawyer loves music and has a huge interest in freedom and dreams. She has a long list of dreams to accomplish, including traveling around the world.

About the author

Flo Fielding is an award-winning, Yorkshire-born writer of dual heritage (Barbadian/English), and a self-confessed "book nerd". Flo writes children's books about identity and family life, and is passionate about children seeing themselves and their families represented in the stories they read. Flo lives in London with her husband, two children, and an extremely shy and fluffy cat.

About Woke Babies

Woke Babies is a children's book subscription box service founded by Kelly-Jade Nicholls. Its mission is to awaken and inspire a love of reading in children through the use of diverse and enjoyable literature. It believes that when children are represented positively in stories—heroes, scientists, or simply as the central focus of a great tale—they're given the chance to envision themselves achieving great things. Woke Babies is dedicated to promoting this kind of inclusivity in children's literature and encouraging every child to feel empowered and confident!

Published by Dorling Kindersley Ltd in association with Woke Babies Ltd

Written by Flo Fielding
Illustrated by Sawyer Cloud
STEM Consultant Joalda Morancy
Educational Consultant Shareen Wilkinson

Editor Abi Luscombe
US Senior Editor Shannon Beatty
Designer Brandie Tully-Scott
Senior Art Editor Charlotte Bull
Publishing Assistant Rea Pikula
Managing Editor Penny Smith
Jacket Coordinator Magda Pszuk
Production Editor Becky Fallowfield
Senior Production Controller Ena Matagic
Publisher Francesca Young
Deputy Art Director Mabel Chan
Publishing Director Sarah Larter

First American Edition, 2023
Published in the United States by DK Publishing
1745 Broadway, 20th Floor, New York, NY 10019

A catalog record for this book
is available from the Library of Congress.
ISBN 978-0-7440-8043-8

DK books are available at special discounts when purchased
in bulk for sales promotions, premiums, fund-raising, or educational
use. For details, contact: DK Publishing Special Markets,
1745 Broadway, 20th Floor, New York, NY 10019
SpecialSales@dk.com

Printed and bound in China

For the curious
www.dk.com

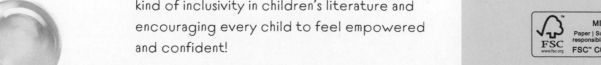

MIX
Paper | Supporting
responsible forestry
FSC™ C018179

This book was made with Forest
Stewardship Council™ certified
paper – one small step in DK's
commitment to a sustainable future.
For more information go to
www.dk.com/our-green-pledge